THERE'S NO COFFEEHOUSE LIKE YOUR HOUSE.

100 of the best coffee recipes you'll find anywhere.

Editors and Content: Meghan Reilly, Kenzie Swanhart, Elizabeth Skladany, and Daniel Davis

Recipe Development: Judy Cannon and Great Flavors Recipe Development Team

Design and Layout: Talia Mangeym

Copywriter: John Grillo

Creative Director: Lauren Wiernasz

Photo Direction: Lauren Wiernasz and Talia Mangeym

Photography: Michael Piazza

Published in the United States of America by
SharkNinja LLC
180 Wells Avenue
Newton, MA 02459

CF090 series ISBN: 978-1-5323-0745-4

10   9   8   7   6   5   4

Printed in China

THE PERKS OF BREWING IT YOURSELF.

Finally, someone who can consistently brew your coffee just the way you like it and spell your name correctly on the cup: **YOU**. With the Ninja Coffee Bar® brewing system, you have everything you need to make all your coffeehouse favorites—not to mention a variety of soon-to-be favorites you can't get anywhere else—all in the comfort of your own home.

MENU

BREWING BASICS

SPECIALTY

HOT

CLASSIC & RICH

CAFE FORTE

COCKTAILS

COLD

ICED COFFEE

ICED & FROZEN SPECIALTY

COCKTAILS

SWEETS

COFFEE COMPLEMENTS

SOFIA'S SIGNATURES

FAVORITE RECIPES

Look for Sofia's signature recipes and personal quotes sprinkled throughout the book. S

SOFIA VERGARA

ACTRESS

COFFEE LOVER

HOME COFFEE BAR-ISTA

Coffee has been in my blood since I was a little girl. Which is why I get so excited when I tell people about the Ninja Coffee Bar®. No matter what type of coffee drink I'm craving—Classic, Rich, Over Ice, or Specialty—I can make it the way I want, when I want. And now with the addition of Ninja's exclusive Cafe Forte brew, plus hot and cold frothing capabilities, I can make drinks at home that aren't available anywhere else. Not even at a coffeehouse.

Sofia

THE BRAINS BEHIND THE BREWS

ADVANCED THERMAL FLAVOR EXTRACTION® TECHNOLOGY

Ninja's patent-pending brewing technology is designed to deliver hot, great-tasting coffee with variable richness levels that are never bitter. Only the Ninja Coffee Bar® has Advanced Thermal Flavor Extraction, which truly unlocks the full flavor potential of your coffee using automated controls for:

- Temperature Calibration
- Pre-Infusion
- Optimal Coffee Saturation Time

BREW TYPES

This unique brewing technology knows just the right amount of flavor to extract to achieve just the strength you want.

Ninja® Custom Brews

CLASSIC BREW

Smooth, balanced flavor from your favorite coffee.

RICH BREW

A more intense flavor than Classic to stand up to milk.

❄ OVER ICE BREW

Richer concentrate designed to brew hot over ice.

Ninja® Signature Brews

SPECIALTY (CONCENTRATED) 4oz

Super-rich concentrate for coffeehouse-style drinks.

CAFE FORTE ⬤ 8oz ⬤

Full-bodied flavors best served black or with a touch of frothed milk.

VARIABLE RICHNESS.
ENDLESS DELISH-NESS.

With the Ninja Coffee Bar® brewer's variable richness settings, you've got endless options for deliciousness ahead of you.

NINJA CUSTOM BREWS

CLASSIC

Hot, smooth
Balanced flavor

RICH

More intense
flavor than Classic

Stands up to milk,
cream, and flavorings

OVER ICE

Deep color, rich flavor—
not watered down

Brews fresh, hot coffee
over ice to lock in flavor

Delicious, distinctive aroma

CAFE FORTE

Super-smooth

Full-bodied, complex flavors

Tastes great black or with
a touch of frothed milk

SPECIALTY

Strongest, richest flavor

Concentrated coffee delivers
the perfect hot, iced, and frozen
blended coffeehouse-style drinks

FROTH IT LIKE IT'S HOT. OR COLD.

Our second-generation Ninja Coffee Bar® takes frothing to a whole new level, transforming milk into a velvety-smooth—**hot or cold**—foam topping for all your favorite indulgent coffee drinks.

AU LAIT

For a smooth finish to our Cafe Forte brew—or any Ninja® Custom Brew—just add 1-3 ounces of frothed milk.

MILK-BASED SPECIALTY

When combined with milk or froth, our Specialty brew creates all your favorite hot and cold layered coffee drinks.

CLASSIC & RICH

Our Classic Brew delivers smooth, balanced flavor from your favorite coffee. Want to take it up a notch? Rich Brew is richer than Classic for a more intense flavor that really stands up to extra milk and flavorings.

CLASSIC/RICH AU LAIT

Classic or Rich brew paired with 1–3 ounces of hot frothed milk.

OVER ICE

Brewed at twice the concentration level of our Classic Brew, Over Ice is designed to brew hot directly over ice—leaving you with a refreshingly cold coffee that's never watered down.

OVER ICE AU LAIT

Over Ice Brew paired with 1–3 ounces of cold frothed milk.

CAFE FORTE

Enjoyed black or with a touch of frothed milk, this exclusive Ninja Coffee Bar® brew is ultra-rich and extra-flavorful. A great after-dinner drink with no bitter aftertaste.

FORTE AU LAIT

Cafe Forte paired with 1–3 ounces of hot frothed milk.

SPECIALTY

Barista, schmarista. Our Specialty brew creates a super-rich concentrate you can use to make all sorts of coffeehouse-style hot and cold layered drinks right in your own home.

GROUNDS
FOR
PERFECTION.

FRESH BEANS

For the most flavorful coffee, it's best to grind fresh whole beans right before you brew.

MEDIUM GRIND

We suggest using a medium grind for the Ninja Coffee Bar® and then adjusting to your liking.

FILTERED WATER

Using fresh, filtered water is recommended for the best flavor.

THE SCOOP ON SCOOPS

We've included this smart double-sided scoop for easy, accurate measuring for any size or brew type.

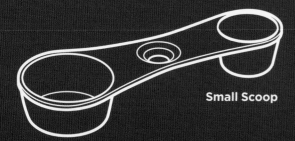

Small Scoop

Big Scoop

SERVING SIZE		NINJA® SCOOP	TABLESPOONS
	CUP/ XL CUP	2-3 Small Scoops	2-3 Tbsp.
	TRAVEL/ XL MULTI-SERVE	4-5 Small Scoops	4-5 Tbsp.
	HALF CARAFE	3-4 Big Scoops	6-8 Tbsp.
	FULL CARAFE	4-6 Big Scoops	8-12 Tbsp.

NINJA SIGNATURE BREWS	NINJA SCOOP	TABLESPOONS
4 OZ. SPECIALTY	2 Big Scoops	4 Tbsp.
8 OZ. CAFE FORTE	2 Big Scoops	4 Tbsp.

VERY VANILLA COFFEE

Size: Travel setting
Brew: Classic
Makes: 1 (16-ounce) serving

INGREDIENTS

4 Ninja® Small Scoops
(or 4 tablespoons)
ground coffee

2 tablespoons
French vanilla syrup

¼ cup half & half

DIRECTIONS

1. Following the measurement provided, place the ground coffee into the brew basket.

2. Place vanilla syrup and half & half into a large mug; set mug in place to brew.

3. Select the Travel size; press the Classic Brew button.

4. When brew is complete, stir to combine.

XL

RICH BREW

CREAMY RASPBERRY COFFEE

Size: XL Cup setting
Brew: Rich
Makes: 1 (14-ounce) serving

INGREDIENTS

3 Ninja® Small Scoops
(or 3 tablespoons)
ground chocolate
raspberry coffee

2 tablespoons vanilla syrup

3 tablespoons half & half

DIRECTIONS

1. Following the measurement provided, place the ground coffee into the brew basket.

2. Place vanilla syrup and half & half into a mug; set mug in place to brew.

3. Select the XL Cup size; press the Rich Brew button.

4. When brew is complete, stir to combine.

CINNAMON TOAST COFFEE

Size: XL Multi-Serve setting
Brew: Classic
Makes: 1 (22-ounce) serving

INGREDIENTS

5 Ninja® Small Scoops
(or 5 tablespoons)
ground coffee

½ teaspoon ground cinnamon

3 tablespoons vanilla syrup

3 tablespoons half & half

DIRECTIONS

1. Following the measurements provided, place the ground coffee and cinnamon into the brew basket.
2. Place vanilla syrup and half & half into 22-ounce or larger travel mug; set mug in place to brew.
3. Select the XL Multi-Serve size; press the Classic Brew button.
4. When brew is complete, stir to combine.

CREAMY BLUEBERRY COFFEE

Size: Cup setting
Brew: Classic
Makes: 1 (13-ounce) serving

INGREDIENTS

3 Ninja® Small Scoops
(or 3 tablespoons)
ground coffee

1 tablespoon blueberry tea leaves

2 tablespoons vanilla syrup

1/4 cup half & half

DIRECTIONS

1. Following the measurements provided, place the ground coffee and blueberry tea leaves into the brew basket.

2. Place vanilla syrup and half & half into a mug; set mug in place to brew.

3. Select the Cup size; press the Classic Brew button.

4. When brew is complete, stir to combine.

CREAMY CHOCOLATE RASPBERRY COFFEE

Size: XL Cup setting
Brew: Rich
Makes: 1 (14-ounce) serving

INGREDIENTS

3 Ninja® Small Scoops
(or 3 tablespoons)
ground chocolate
raspberry coffee

3 tablespoons vanilla syrup

¼ cup half & half

DIRECTIONS

1. Following the measurement provided, place the ground coffee into the brew basket.
2. Place vanilla syrup and half & half into a mug; set mug in place to brew.
3. Select the XL Cup size; press the Rich Brew button.
4. When brew is complete, stir to combine.

CLASSIC & RICH

RICH BREW

CARAMEL PECAN COFFEE

Size: Full Carafe setting
Brew: Rich
Makes: 4 (12-ounce) servings

INGREDIENTS

6 Ninja® Big Scoops
(or 12 tablespoons)
ground pecan-flavored coffee

1/3 cup caramel syrup

1/3 cup chocolate syrup

1/4 teaspoon salt

1 cup half & half

DIRECTIONS

1. Following the measurement provided, place the ground coffee into the brew basket.

2. Place caramel syrup, chocolate syrup, and salt into the carafe; set carafe in place to brew.

3. Select the Full Carafe size; press the Rich Brew button.

4. While coffee is brewing, place half & half into a large mug.

5. When brew is complete, stir to combine.

6. Microwave half & half for 30 to 45 seconds. Froth for 30 seconds according to frothing instructions in the Owner's Guide.

7. Pour coffee into 4 mugs. Gently pour frothed half & half into coffee.

SOFIA'S SIGNATURE

"This is such a treat to drink any time of the day."

CAFE CON CHOCOLATE COFFEE

Size: Half Carafe setting
Brew: Rich
Makes: 4 (8-ounce) servings

INGREDIENTS

3 Ninja® Big Scoops
(or 6 tablespoons)
ground coffee

2 packets hot chocolate mix

1 $\frac{1}{2}$ cups milk, warm, divided

Whipped cream, for garnish

Chocolate syrup, for garnish

DIRECTIONS

1. Following the measurement provided, place the ground coffee into the brew basket.

2. In a measuring cup, stir together hot chocolate mix and $\frac{1}{2}$ cup milk until well combined. Stir in remaining milk and mix well.

3. Pour hot chocolate mixture into the carafe; set carafe in place to brew.

4. Select the Half Carafe size; press the Rich Brew button.

5. When brew is complete, gently stir to combine and divide between 4 cups. Top with whipped cream and drizzle with chocolate syrup.

TOO GOOD TOFFEE COFFEE

Size: Cup setting
Brew: Rich
Makes: 1 (12-ounce) serving

INGREDIENTS

3 Ninja® Small Scoops
(or 3 tablespoons)
ground coffee

1 tablespoon butterscotch
or caramel sauce

1 tablespoon dark brown sugar

1/4 teaspoon vanilla extract

1/8 teaspoon salt

1/4 cup heavy cream

DIRECTIONS

1. Following the measurement provided, place the ground coffee into the brew basket.

2. Place butterscotch or caramel sauce, brown sugar, vanilla extract, and salt into a mug; set mug in place to brew.

3. Select the Cup size; press the Rich Brew button.

4. While coffee is brewing, place cream into another mug.

5. When brew is complete, stir to combine.

6. Microwave cream for 30 to 45 seconds. Froth for 30 seconds according to frothing instructions in the Owner's Guide.

7. Gently pour frothed cream into coffee.

MILK & HONEY COFFEE

Size: Travel setting
Brew: Classic
Makes: 1 (16-ounce) serving

INGREDIENTS

4 Ninja® Small Scoops
(or 4 tablespoons)
ground coffee

2 tablespoons honey

¼ cup half & half

DIRECTIONS

1. Following the measurement provided, place the ground coffee into the brew basket.

2. Place honey and half & half into a microwave-safe travel mug. Microwave for 30 seconds, then set mug in place to brew.

3. Select the Travel size; press the Classic Brew button.

4. When brew is complete, stir to combine.

SOFIA'S SIGNATURE

"Perfect for a subtly sweet morning drink."

Sofia

CINNAMON GRAHAM COFFEE

Size: XL Multi-Serve setting
Brew: Classic
Makes: 1 (22-ounce) serving

INGREDIENTS

5 Ninja® Small Scoops
(or 5 tablespoons)
ground coffee

1/2 teaspoon ground cinnamon

1 teaspoon molasses

1 teaspoon honey

1/2 cup half & half

1/4 cup marshmallow topping

2 teaspoons vanilla extract

4 teaspoons cinnamon graham
crackers, crushed, for garnish

DIRECTIONS

1. Following the measurement provided, place the ground coffee into the brew basket.

2. Place cinnamon, molasses, and honey into a 22-ounce or larger travel mug; set mug in place to brew.

3. Select the XL Multi-Serve size; press the Classic Brew button.

4. While coffee is brewing, place half & half, marshmallow topping, and vanilla extract into a large mug.

5. When brew is complete, stir to combine. Then split coffee between 2 mugs.

6. Microwave half & half mixture for 30 to 45 seconds. Froth for 30 seconds according to frothing instructions in the Owner's Guide.

7. Gently pour frothed mixture into the 2 mugs of coffee and sprinkle with crushed cinnamon graham crackers.

LICORICE OVER LOUISIANA COFFEE

Size: XL Cup setting
Brew: Rich
Makes: 1 (16-ounce) serving

INGREDIENTS

3 Ninja® Small Scoops
(or 3 tablespoons)
ground coffee & chicory blend

2 teaspoons anise seed

1 teaspoon sugar

½ cup milk

DIRECTIONS

1. Following the measurements provided, place the ground coffee & chicory blend and anise seed into the brew basket.

2. Place sugar into a large mug; set mug in place to brew.

3. Select the XL Cup size; press the Rich Brew button.

4. While coffee is brewing, place milk into another large mug.

5. When brew is complete, stir to combine.

6. Microwave milk for 30 to 45 seconds. Froth for 30 seconds according to frothing instructions in the Owner's Guide.

7. Gently pour frothed milk into coffee.

CRÈME DE CARAMEL COFFEE

Size: Travel setting
Brew: Classic
Makes: 1 (16-ounce) serving

INGREDIENTS

4 Ninja® Small Scoops
(or 4 tablespoons)
ground coffee

2 tablespoons caramel syrup

¼ cup half & half

DIRECTIONS

1. Following the measurement provided, place the ground coffee into the brew basket.

2. Place the caramel syrup and half & half into a large mug. Microwave for 30 seconds, then set mug in place to brew.

3. Select the Travel size; press the Classic Brew button.

4. When brew is complete, stir to combine.

COCONUT HAZELNUT COFFEE

Size: Cup setting
Brew: Rich
Makes: 1 (10-ounce) serving

INGREDIENTS

3 Ninja® Small Scoops
(or 3 tablespoons)
ground coconut coffee

2 tablespoons hazelnut syrup

2 tablespoons half & half

DIRECTIONS

1. Following the measurement provided, place the ground coffee into the brew basket.

2. Place hazelnut syrup and half & half into a mug; set mug in place to brew.

3. Select the Cup size; press the Rich Brew button.

4. When brew is complete, stir to combine.

CHOCOLATE COVERED PRETZEL COFFEE

Size: XL Cup setting
Brew: Rich
Makes: 1 (16-ounce) serving

INGREDIENTS

3 Ninja® Small Scoops
(or 3 tablespoons)
ground coffee

1 tablespoon crushed pretzel

2 tablespoons chocolate
hazelnut spread

1/8 teaspoon salt

1/4 cup half & half

DIRECTIONS

1. Following the measurements provided, place the ground coffee and crushed pretzel into the brew basket.
2. Place the chocolate hazelnut spread and salt into a large mug; set mug in place to brew.
3. Select the XL Cup size; press the Rich Brew button.
4. While coffee is brewing, place the half & half into another large mug.
5. When brew is complete, stir to combine.
6. Microwave half & half for 30 to 45 seconds. Froth for 30 seconds according to frothing instructions in the Owner's Guide.
7. Gently pour frothed half & half into brewed coffee.

MOCHA HAZELNUT DELIGHT COFFEE

Size: Cup setting
Brew: Classic
Makes: 1 (13-ounce) serving

INGREDIENTS

3 Ninja® Small Scoops
(or 3 tablespoons)
ground coffee

2 tablespoons chocolate syrup

2 tablespoons hazelnut syrup

¼ cup milk

DIRECTIONS

1. Following the measurement provided, place the ground coffee into the brew basket.

2. Place chocolate syrup, hazelnut syrup, and milk into a large mug; set mug in place to brew.

3. Select the Cup size; press the Classic Brew button.

4. When brew is complete, stir to combine.

HAZELNUT BRITTLE COFFEE

Size: Full Carafe setting
Brew: Rich
Makes: 4 (14-ounce) servings

INGREDIENTS

6 Ninja® Big Scoops
(or 12 tablespoons)
ground hazelnut coffee

1/2 cup butterscotch syrup

3/4 cup heavy cream

1/2 teaspoon salt

DIRECTIONS

1. Following the measurement provided, place the ground coffee into the brew basket.
2. Place butterscotch syrup, cream, and salt into the carafe; set carafe in place to brew.
3. Select the Full Carafe size; press the Rich Brew button.
4. When brew is complete, stir to combine and divide between 4 mugs.

CLASSIC BREW

SALTED CARAMEL COFFEE

Size: Cup setting
Brew: Classic
Makes: 1 (12-ounce) serving

INGREDIENTS

3 Ninja® Small Scoops
(or 3 tablespoons)
ground coffee

2 tablespoons caramel syrup

2 tablespoons half & half

Dash sea salt

DIRECTIONS

1. Following the measurement provided, place the ground coffee into the brew basket.

2. Place caramel syrup, half & half, and salt into a mug; set mug in place to brew.

3. Select the Cup size; press the Classic Brew button.

4. When brew is complete, stir to combine.

PEPPERMINT VANILLA COFFEE

Size: Cup setting
Brew: Classic
Makes: 1 (12-ounce) serving

INGREDIENTS

3 Ninja® Small Scoops
(or 3 tablespoons)
ground French vanilla coffee

3 tablespoons vanilla syrup

1 drop peppermint extract

2 tablespoons half & half

DIRECTIONS

1. Following the measurement provided, place the ground coffee into the brew basket.
2. Place vanilla syrup, peppermint extract, and half & half into a mug; set mug in place to brew.
3. Select the Cup size; press the Classic Brew button.
4. When brew is complete, stir to combine.

CLASSIC & RICH

RICH BREW

LAVENDER LUXE COFFEE

Size: Cup setting
Brew: Rich
Makes: 1 (13-ounce) serving

INGREDIENTS

3 Ninja® Small Scoops
(or 3 tablespoons)
ground coffee

1 teaspoon dried lavender,
plus pinch for garnish

½ cup milk

1 tablespoon honey

DIRECTIONS

1. Following the measurements provided, stir together the ground coffee and dried lavender; place into the brew basket.

2. Set a large mug in place to brew.

3. Select the Cup size; press the Rich Brew button.

4. While coffee is brewing, place milk and honey into another large mug.

5. When brew is complete, stir to combine.

6. Microwave milk mixture for 30 to 45 seconds. Froth for 30 seconds according to frothing instructions in the Owner's Guide.

7. Gently pour frothed mixture into coffee and sprinkle with dried lavender.

MEXICAN SPICED COFFEE

Size: Half Carafe setting
Brew: Rich
Makes: 2 (7-ounce) servings

INGREDIENTS

3 Ninja® Big Scoops
(or 6 tablespoons)
ground coffee

1 teaspoon ground cinnamon

$1/2$ teaspoon chili powder

$1/4$ teaspoon cayenne pepper

$1/4$ cup heavy cream

1 tablespoon unsweetened
cocoa powder

1 tablespoon confectioners' sugar

DIRECTIONS

1. Following the measurements provided, stir together the ground coffee, cinnamon, chili powder, and cayenne pepper; place into the brew basket.

2. Set the carafe in place to brew.

3. Select the Half Carafe size; press the Rich Brew button.

4. While coffee is brewing, whip heavy cream with cocoa and confectioners' sugar until soft peaks form.

5. When brew is complete, pour coffee into 2 mugs and top each with the whipped cream.

MAPLE PECAN COFFEE

Size: Full Carafe setting
Brew: Classic
Makes: 4 (12-ounce) servings

INGREDIENTS

6 Ninja® Big Scoops
(or 12 tablespoons) ground
pecan-flavored coffee

½ cup heavy cream

2 tablespoons maple syrup

½ teaspoon ground cinnamon,
plus more for garnish

DIRECTIONS

1. Following the measurement provided, place the ground coffee into the brew basket.

2. Set the carafe in place to brew.

3. Select the Full Carafe size; press the Classic Brew button.

4. While coffee is brewing, whip heavy cream with maple syrup and cinnamon until soft peaks form.

5. When brew is complete, pour coffee into 4 mugs. Top each with whipped cream and cinnamon.

RED VELVET COFFEE

Size: XL Cup setting
Brew: Rich
Makes: 1 (16-ounce) serving

INGREDIENTS

3 Ninja® Small Scoops
(or 3 tablespoons)
ground coffee

3 chocolate sandwich cookies,
chopped

$1/8$ teaspoon vanilla extract

$1/4$ cup half & half

1 tablespoon sugar

2 tablespoons (1 ounce)
cream cheese

DIRECTIONS

1. Following the measurement provided, place the ground coffee into the brew basket.

2. Add chocolate sandwich cookies and vanilla to a large mug; set mug in place to brew.

3. Select the XL Cup size; press the Rich Brew button.

4. While coffee is brewing, place half & half, sugar, and cream cheese into another large mug and stir to combine.

5. When brew is complete, stir to combine coffee, cookies, and vanilla.

6. Microwave half & half mixture for 30 to 45 seconds. Froth for 30 seconds according to frothing instructions in the Owner's Guide.

7. Gently pour frothed mixture into coffee.

ORANGE MOCHA COFFEE

Size: Full Carafe setting
Brew: Rich
Makes: 4 (12-ounce) servings

INGREDIENTS

6 Ninja® Big Scoops
(or 12 tablespoons)
ground coffee

Peel from 1 $1/2$ oranges,
pith removed

$3/4$ cup chocolate syrup

1 cup half & half

DIRECTIONS

1. Following the measurement provided, place the ground coffee into the brew basket.
2. Place orange peel and chocolate syrup into the carafe; set carafe in place to brew.
3. Select the Full Carafe size; press the Rich Brew button.
4. While coffee is brewing, place half & half into a large mug.
5. When brew is complete, stir to combine.
6. Microwave half & half for 30 to 45 seconds. Froth for 30 seconds according to frothing instructions in the Owner's Guide.
7. Divide coffee between 4 mugs, then gently pour in frothed mixture.

PIÑA COLADA COFFEE

Size: XL Cup setting
Brew: Rich
Makes: 1 (16-ounce) serving

INGREDIENTS

3 Ninja® Small Scoops
(or 3 tablespoons)
ground coffee

¼ cup fresh or canned
pineapple, crushed

½ cup coconut milk

¼ cup sweetened
condensed milk

Toasted sweetened coconut,
for garnish

Sliced pineapple, for garnish

DIRECTIONS

1. Following the measurements provided, place the ground coffee and pineapple into the brew basket.

2. Set a large mug in place to brew.

3. Select the XL Cup size; press the Rich Brew button.

4. While coffee is brewing, place coconut milk and sweetened condensed milk into another large mug.

5. When brew is complete, stir to combine.

6. Microwave milk for 30 to 45 seconds. Froth for 30 seconds according to frothing instructions in the Owner's Guide.

7. Gently pour frothed mixture into coffee. Garnish with toasted coconut and sliced pineapple.

SPECIALTY
(CONCENTRATED)
4oz

CAPPUCCINO-STYLE COFFEE

Brew: Specialty
Makes: 1 (12-ounce) serving

INGREDIENTS

2 Ninja® Big Scoops
(or 4 tablespoons)
ground coffee

½ cup milk

Ground cinnamon,
for garnish

DIRECTIONS

1. Place milk into a large mug. Microwave for 30 to 45 seconds. Froth for 30 seconds according to frothing instructions in the Owner's Guide.

2. Following the measurement provided, place the ground coffee into the brew basket.

3. Set the mug containing frothed milk in place to brew.

4. Press the Specialty button.

5. When brew is complete, sweeten as desired. Garnish with a sprinkle of cinnamon.

PUMPKIN SPICE LATTE

SPECIALTY
(CONCENTRATED)
4oz

Brew: Specialty
Makes: 1 (12-ounce) serving

INGREDIENTS

2 Ninja® Big Scoops
(or 4 tablespoons)
ground coffee

$\frac{1}{2}$ cup milk

1 tablespoon dark brown sugar

$\frac{1}{4}$ teaspoon pumpkin pie spice,
plus more for garnish

Pinch salt

DIRECTIONS

1. Following the measurement provided, place the ground coffee into the brew basket.

2. Set a mug in place to brew.

3. Press the Specialty button.

4. While coffee is brewing, place milk, brown sugar, pumpkin pie spice, and salt into a large mug.

5. When brew is complete, microwave milk mixture for 30 to 45 seconds. Froth for 20 to 30 seconds according to frothing instructions in the Owner's Guide.

6. Gently pour frothed mixture into coffee. Sprinkle with additional pumpkin pie spice.

ALMOND MILK LATTE

Brew: Specialty
Makes: 1 (10-ounce) serving

INGREDIENTS

2 Ninja® Big Scoops
(or 4 tablespoons)
ground coffee

2 tablespoons vanilla syrup

$\frac{1}{2}$ cup almond milk

DIRECTIONS

1. Following the measurement provided, place the ground coffee into the brew basket.

2. Place vanilla syrup into a mug; set mug in place to brew.

3. Press the Specialty button.

4. While coffee is brewing, place almond milk into another mug.

5. When brew is complete, stir to combine.

6. Microwave milk for 30 to 45 seconds. Froth for 20 to 30 seconds according to frothing instructions in the Owner's Guide.

7. Gently pour frothed almond milk into coffee.

SOFIA'S
SIGNATURE
"Lattes can be delicious
even without dairy."

Sofia

CARAMEL NUTMEG LATTE

Brew: Specialty
Makes: 1 (10-ounce) serving

INGREDIENTS

2 Ninja® Big Scoops
(or 4 tablespoons)
ground coffee

$\frac{1}{2}$ teaspoon ground nutmeg,
plus more for garnish

2 tablespoons caramel syrup

$\frac{1}{2}$ cup milk

DIRECTIONS

1. Following the measurements provided, place the ground coffee and nutmeg into the brew basket.

2. Place caramel syrup into a mug; set mug in place to brew.

3. Press the Specialty button.

4. While coffee is brewing, place milk into another mug.

5. When brew is complete, stir to combine.

6. Microwave milk for 30 to 45 seconds. Froth for 20 to 30 seconds according to frothing instructions in the Owner's Guide.

7. Gently pour frothed milk into coffee. Sprinkle with additional nutmeg.

SPECIALTY
(CONCENTRATED)
4oz

MARSHMALLOW MINT LATTE

Brew: Specialty
Makes: 1 (10-ounce) serving

INGREDIENTS

2 Ninja® Big Scoops
(or 4 tablespoons)
ground coffee

3 squares chocolate-mint
sandwich candy, chopped

1/2 cup milk

1/4 cup marshmallow cream

DIRECTIONS

1. Following the measurement provided, place the ground coffee into the brew basket.
2. Place the chocolate-mint candy into a large mug; set mug in place to brew.
3. Press the Specialty button.
4. While coffee is brewing, place milk and marshmallow cream into another large mug and stir to combine.
5. When brew is complete, stir to combine.
6. Microwave milk mixture for 30 to 45 seconds. Froth for 20 to 30 seconds according to frothing instructions in the Owner's Guide.
7. Gently pour frothed mixture into coffee.

FLAT WHITE

Brew: Specialty
Makes: 1 (10-ounce) serving

INGREDIENTS

2 Ninja® Big Scoops
(or 4 tablespoons)
ground coffee

½ cup milk

DIRECTIONS

1. Following the measurement provided, place the ground coffee into the brew basket.

2. Set a mug in place to brew.

3. Press the Specialty button.

4. While coffee is brewing, place milk into another mug.

5. When brew is complete, microwave milk for 30 to 45 seconds. Froth for 30 seconds according to frothing instructions in the Owner's Guide.

6. Pour frothed milk into coffee, using a spoon to hold back the large foam. Then top coffee with a dollop of large foam.

SPECIALTY
(CONCENTRATED)
4oz

CINNAMON MOCHA LATTE

Brew: Specialty
Makes: 1 (10-ounce) serving

INGREDIENTS

2 Ninja® Big Scoops
(or 4 tablespoons)
ground coffee

½ teaspoon ground cinnamon,
plus more for garnish

2 tablespoons chocolate syrup

½ cup milk

DIRECTIONS

1. Following the measurements provided, place the ground coffee and cinnamon into the brew basket.

2. Place chocolate syrup into a mug; set mug in place to brew.

3. Press the Specialty button.

4. While coffee is brewing, place milk into another mug.

5. When brew is complete, stir to combine.

6. Microwave milk for 30 to 45 seconds. Froth for 20 to 30 seconds according to frothing instructions in the Owner's Guide.

7. Gently pour frothed milk into coffee. Sprinkle with additional cinnamon.

SILK ROAD COFFEE

Brew: Specialty
Makes: 1 (10-ounce) serving

INGREDIENTS

2 Ninja® Big Scoops
(or 4 tablespoons)
ground coffee

³/₄ teaspoon ground ginger

³/₄ teaspoon ground cinnamon

¹/₂ teaspoon ground cardamom

¹/₄ teaspoon ground nutmeg

¹/₄ teaspoon ground black pepper

¹/₈ teaspoon ground cloves

¹/₂ cup milk

1 tablespoon French vanilla syrup

Cracked black pepper,
for garnish

DIRECTIONS

1. Following the measurements provided, stir together the ground coffee and spices; place into the brew basket.

2. Set a mug in place to brew.

3. Press the Specialty button.

4. While coffee is brewing, place milk and vanilla syrup into a large mug.

5. When brew is complete, stir to combine.

6. Microwave milk mixture for 30 to 45 seconds. Froth for 30 seconds according to frothing instructions in the Owner's Guide.

7. Gently pour frothed mixture into coffee and sprinkle with cracked black pepper.

CARAMEL MACCHIATO FORTE

Brew: Cafe Forte
Makes: 1 (12-ounce) serving

INGREDIENTS

2 Ninja® Big Scoops
(or 4 tablespoons)
ground coffee

3 tablespoons caramel sauce,
plus more for garnish

2 tablespoons milk

DIRECTIONS

1. Following the measurement provided, place the ground coffee into the brew basket.
2. Place caramel sauce into a large mug. Set mug in place to brew.
3. Press the Cafe Forte button.
4. While coffee is brewing, place milk into another large mug.
5. When brew is complete, stir to combine.
6. Microwave milk for 20 seconds. Froth for 30 seconds according to frothing instructions in the Owner's Guide.
7. Gently pour frothed into coffee. Drizzle with additional caramel sauce.

SOFIA'S SIGNATURE

"This recipe had me at caramel."

FORTE
AU LAIT

Brew: Cafe Forte
Makes: 1 (12-ounce) serving

INGREDIENTS

2 Ninja® Big Scoops
(or 4 tablespoons)
ground coffee

⅓ cup milk

DIRECTIONS

1. Following the measurement provided, place the ground coffee into the brew basket.
2. Set a large mug in place to brew.
3. Press the Cafe Forte button.
4. While coffee is brewing, place milk into another large mug.
5. When brew is complete, microwave milk for 30 to 45 seconds. Froth for 30 seconds according to frothing instructions in the Owner's Guide.
6. Gently pour frothed milk into coffee.

CAFE FORTE
8oz

MOLE SPICED FORTE

Brew: Cafe Forte
Makes: 1 (9-ounce) serving

INGREDIENTS

2 Ninja® Big Scoops
(or 4 tablespoons)
ground coffee

1 teaspoon cocoa powder

½ teaspoon ground cinnamon

¼ teaspoon chili powder

⅛ teaspoon cayenne pepper

DIRECTIONS

1. Following the measurements provided, stir together all ingredients; place into the brew basket.

2. Set a large mug in place to brew.

3. Press the Cafe Forte button.

4. When brew is complete, stir to combine.

VIETNAMESE-STYLE FORTE

Brew: Cafe Forte
Makes: 1 (9-ounce) serving

INGREDIENTS

2 Ninja® Big Scoops
(or 4 tablespoons)
ground coffee

$\frac{1}{8}$ teaspoon ground cinnamon

$\frac{1}{8}$ teaspoon ground ginger

$\frac{1}{8}$ teaspoon ground cardamom

1 piece fresh orange peel,
pith removed

1 tablespoon sweetened
condensed milk

DIRECTIONS

1. Following the measurements provided, stir together the ground coffee, cinnamon, ginger, and cardamom; place into the brew basket.

2. Place the orange peel into a large mug; set mug in place to brew.

3. Press the Cafe Forte button.

4. When brew is complete, gently stir in sweetened condensed milk.

CAFE FORTE
8oz

YEMENI GINGER FORTE

Brew: Cafe Forte
Makes: 1 (16-ounce) serving

INGREDIENTS

2 Ninja® Big Scoops
(or 4 tablespoons)
ground coffee

1 tablespoon finely grated ginger

1 cinnamon stick

1 teaspoon palm sugar

DIRECTIONS

1. Following the measurements provided, stir together the ground coffee and ginger; place into the brew basket.

2. Place the cinnamon stick and sugar into a large mug; set mug in place to brew.

3. Press the Cafe Forte button.

4. When brew is complete, stir to combine.

CAFE FORTE
8oz

SALTED MOCHA FORTE AU LAIT

Brew: Cafe Forte
Makes: 1 (12-ounce) serving

INGREDIENTS

2 Ninja® Big Scoops
(or 4 tablespoons)
ground coffee

3 tablespoons chocolate syrup,
plus more for garnish

$\frac{1}{8}$ teaspoon salt

$\frac{1}{4}$ cup milk

DIRECTIONS

1. Following the measurement provided, place the ground coffee into the brew basket.
2. Add chocolate syrup and salt to a large mug; set mug in place to brew.
3. Press the Cafe Forte button.
4. While coffee is brewing, place milk into another large mug.
5. When brew is complete, stir to combine.
6. Microwave milk for 30 to 45 seconds. Froth for 30 seconds according to frothing instructions in the Owner's Guide.
7. Gently pour frothed milk into coffee. Drizzle with chocolate syrup.

CAFE CON MIEL FORTE AU LAIT

Brew: Cafe Forte
Makes: 1 (16-ounce) serving

INGREDIENTS

2 Ninja® Big Scoops
(or 4 tablespoons)
ground coffee

⅓ cup half & half

1 tablespoon honey

¼ teaspoon cinnamon,
plus more for garnish

DIRECTIONS

1. Following the measurement provided, place the ground coffee into the brew basket.

2. Set a large mug in place to brew.

3. Press the Cafe Forte button.

4. While coffee is brewing, place half & half, honey, and cinnamon into another large mug.

5. When brew is complete, microwave half & half mixture for 30 to 45 seconds. Froth for 30 seconds according to frothing instructions in the Owner's Guide.

6. Gently pour frothed mixture into coffee and sprinkle with cinnamon.

SOFIA'S SIGNATURE

"I like to serve this after dinner, but it's a great afternoon pick-me-up too."

Sofia

INDONESIAN FORTE AU LAIT

Brew: Cafe Forte
Makes: 1 (12-ounce) serving

INGREDIENTS

2 Ninja® Big Scoops
(or 4 tablespoons)
ground coffee

2 tablespoons fresh lemongrass, minced

1 tablespoon fresh ginger, thinly sliced

$\frac{1}{4}$ teaspoon cinnamon

$\frac{1}{4}$ teaspoon cardamom

2 teaspoons coconut sugar

$\frac{1}{4}$ cup coconut milk

DIRECTIONS

1. Following the measurements provided, stir together the ground coffee, lemongrass, ginger, cinnamon, and cardamom; place into the brew basket.

2. Set a mug in place to brew.

3. Press the Cafe Forte button.

4. While coffee is brewing, place coconut sugar and coconut milk into another mug.

5. When brew is complete, stir to combine.

6. Microwave milk mixture for 30 to 45 seconds. Froth for 30 seconds according to frothing instructions in the Owner's Guide.

7. Gently pour frothed milk into coffee.

CLASSIC CAFE ROMANO FORTE

Brew: Cafe Forte
Makes: 1 (8-ounce) serving

INGREDIENTS

2 Ninja® Big Scoops
(or 4 tablespoons)
ground coffee

Peel from 1 lemon,
pith removed

DIRECTIONS

1. Following the measurement provided, place the ground coffee into the brew basket.

2. Place the lemon peel into a mug; set mug in place to brew.

3. Press the Cafe Forte button.

CREOLE COFFEE COCKTAIL

Size: Half Carafe setting
Brew: Rich
Makes: 4 (6-ounce) servings

INGREDIENTS

3 Ninja® Big Scoops
(or 6 tablespoons)
ground coffee

2 tablespoons granulated sugar

1/4 cup brandy or cognac

Peel of 1 orange,
pith removed

2 whole cloves

1 cinnamon stick

Whipped cream,
for garnish

DIRECTIONS

1. Following the measurement provided, place the ground coffee into the brew basket.

2. Set the carafe in place to brew.

3. Select the Half Carafe size; press the Rich Brew button.

4. While coffee is brewing, combine sugar, brandy, orange peel, cloves, and cinnamon stick in a small saucepan over low heat, stirring, until sugar dissolves. Discard the orange peel and spices.

5. When brew is complete, pour coffee into 4 mugs, then divide brandy mixture between them. Top with whipped cream.

CAFE FORTE
8oz

IRISH CAFE FORTE

Brew: Cafe Forte
Makes: 1 (14-ounce) serving

INGREDIENTS

2 Ninja® Big Scoops
(or 4 tablespoons)
ground coffee

3 tablespoons whiskey

3 teaspoons dark brown sugar,
divided

1/4 cup heavy cream

DIRECTIONS

1. Following the measurement provided, place the ground coffee into the brew basket.

2. Place the whiskey and 2 teaspoons brown sugar into a large mug; set mug in place to brew.

3. Press the Cafe Forte button.

4. While coffee is brewing, whip heavy cream with 1 teaspoon brown sugar.

5. When brew is complete, stir to combine. Top with the whipped cream.

HAZELNUT ICED COFFEE

Size: Travel setting
Brew: Over Ice
Makes: 1 (16-ounce) serving

INGREDIENTS

4 Ninja® Small Scoops
(or 4 tablespoons)
ground coffee

2 cups ice

3 tablespoons hazelnut syrup

½ cup half & half

DIRECTIONS

1. Following the measurement provided, place the ground coffee into the brew basket.
2. Place the ice, hazelnut syrup, and half & half into a large plastic cup, set cup in place to brew.
3. Select the Travel size; press the Over Ice Brew button.
4. When brew is complete, stir to combine.

FRENCH VANILLA ICED COFFEE

Size: XL Multi-Serve setting
Brew: Over Ice
Makes: 1 (22-ounce) serving

INGREDIENTS

5 Ninja® Small Scoops
(or 5 tablespoons)
ground coffee

2 cups ice

¼ cup French vanilla syrup

¼ cup half & half

DIRECTIONS

1. Following the measurement provided, place the ground coffee into the brew basket.

2. Place ice, vanilla syrup, and half & half into a 22-ounce or larger plastic cup; set cup in place to brew.

3. Select the XL Multi-Serve size; press the Over Ice Brew button.

4. When brew is complete, stir to combine.

MOCHA MINT COOLER

Size: XL Multi-Serve setting
Brew: Over Ice
Makes: 1 (22-ounce) serving

INGREDIENTS

5 Ninja® Small Scoops
(or 5 tablespoons)
ground coconut coffee

$\frac{1}{8}$ teaspoon mint extract

2 cups ice

$\frac{1}{4}$ chocolate syrup

$\frac{1}{4}$ cup milk

DIRECTIONS

1. Following the measurements provided, place the ground coffee and mint extract into the brew basket.

2. Place the ice, chocolate syrup, and milk into a 22-ounce or larger plastic cup; set cup in place to brew.

3. Select the XL Multi-Serve size; press the Over Ice Brew button.

4. When brew is complete, stir to combine.

WHITE CHOCOLATE HAZELNUT ICED COFFEE

Size: Travel setting
Brew: Over Ice
Makes: 1 (16-ounce) serving

INGREDIENTS

4 Ninja® Small Scoops
(or 4 tablespoons)
ground hazelnut coffee

2 cups ice

2 tablespoons
white chocolate syrup

2 tablespoons half & half

DIRECTIONS

1. Following the measurement provided, place the ground coffee into the brew basket.

2. Place the ice, white chocolate syrup, and half & half into a large plastic cup; set cup in place to brew.

3. Select the Travel size; press the Over Ice Brew button.

4. When brew is complete, stir to combine.

BLUEBERRIES & CREAM ICED COFFEE

Size: Travel setting
Brew: Over Ice
Makes: 1 (16-ounce) serving

INGREDIENTS

4 Ninja® Small Scoops
(or 4 tablespoons)
ground blueberry coffee

2 cups ice

2 tablespoons vanilla syrup

2 tablespoons half & half

DIRECTIONS

1. Following the measurement provided, place the ground coffee into the brew basket.
2. Place the ice, vanilla syrup, and half & half into a large plastic cup; set cup in place to brew.
3. Select the Travel size; press the Over Ice Brew button.
4. When brew is complete, stir to combine.

THAI-STYLE ICED COFFEE

Size: XL Cup setting
Brew: Over Ice
Makes: 1 (20-ounce) serving

INGREDIENTS

3 Ninja® Small Scoops
(or 3 tablespoons)
ground coffee

1/3 cup sweetened
condensed milk

1/3 cup milk

2 cups ice

DIRECTIONS

1. Following the measurement provided, place the ground coffee into the brew basket.

2. Combine the milks in a large plastic cup; stir to combine.

3. Add the ice to the cup; set cup in place to brew.

4. Select the XL Cup size; press the Over Ice Brew button.

5. When brew is complete, stir to combine.

GINGERSNAP ICED COFFEE

Size: Travel setting
Brew: Over Ice
Makes: 1 (16-ounce) serving

INGREDIENTS

4 Ninja® Small Scoops
(or 4 tablespoons)
ground coffee

$\frac{1}{2}$ teaspoon ground cinnamon

$\frac{1}{4}$ teaspoon ground ginger

2 cups ice

2 tablespoons vanilla syrup

2 tablespoons half & half

DIRECTIONS

1. Following the measurements provided, place the ground coffee, cinnamon, and ginger into the brew basket.
2. Place the ice, vanilla syrup, and half & half into a large plastic cup; set cup in place to brew.
3. Select the Travel size; press the Over Ice Brew button.
4. When brew is complete, stir to combine.

OVER ICE BREW

CHOCOLATE HAZELNUT ICED COFFEE

Size: Full Carafe setting
Brew: Over Ice
Makes: 4 (13-ounce) servings

INGREDIENTS

6 Ninja® Big Scoops
(or 12 tablespoons)
ground hazelnut coffee

4 cups ice

½ cup chocolate syrup

1 cup half & half

DIRECTIONS

1. Following the measurement provided, place the ground coffee into the brew basket.

2. Place the ice, chocolate syrup, and half & half into the carafe; set carafe in place to brew.

3. Select the Full Carafe size; press the Over Ice Brew button.

4. When brew is complete, stir to combine. Pour coffee into 4 glasses.

MAPLE CHICORY OVER ICE AU LAIT

Size: Cup setting
Brew: Over Ice
Makes: 1 (18-ounce) serving

INGREDIENTS

3 Ninja® Small Scoops
(or 3 tablespoons)
ground coffee & chicory blend

2 cups ice

2 teaspoons maple syrup

⅓ cup milk

DIRECTIONS

1. Following the measurement provided, place the ground coffee into the brew basket.
2. Place the ice and maple syrup into a large plastic cup; set cup in place to brew.
3. Select the Cup size; press the Over Ice Brew button.
4. While coffee is brewing, place milk into a mug.
5. When brew is complete, stir to combine. Froth milk for 30 seconds according to frothing instructions in the Owner's Guide.
6. Gently pour frothed milk into coffee.

SOFIA'S SIGNATURE

"A refreshing taste of New Orleans in every sip."

Sofia

CINNAMON CARAMEL ICED COFFEE

Size: Travel setting
Brew: Over Ice
Makes: 1 (16-ounce) serving

INGREDIENTS

4 Ninja® Small Scoops
(or 4 tablespoons)
ground coffee

$\frac{1}{2}$ teaspoon ground cinnamon

2 cups ice

2 tablespoons caramel syrup

2 tablespoons half & half

DIRECTIONS

1. Following the measurements provided, place the ground coffee and cinnamon into the brew basket.

2. Place the ice, caramel syrup, and half & half into a large plastic cup; set cup in place to brew.

3. Select the Travel size; press the Over Ice Brew button.

4. When brew is complete, stir to combine.

ORANGE CREAM ICED COFFEE

Size: Half Carafe setting
Brew: Over Ice
Makes: 4 (9-ounce) servings

INGREDIENTS

3 Ninja® Big Scoops
(or 6 tablespoons)
ground coffee

3 cups ice

Peel of 1 orange,
pith removed

1 teaspoon vanilla bean paste
(or 2 teaspoons vanilla extract)

2 tablespoons
plus 2 teaspoons sugar

$3/4$ cup heavy cream

DIRECTIONS

1. Following the measurement provided, place the ground coffee into the brew basket.

2. Place the ice, orange peel, vanilla, sugar, and heavy cream into the carafe; set carafe in place to brew.

3. Select the Half Carafe size; press the Over Ice Brew button.

4. When brew is complete, stir to combine. Pour coffee into 4 glasses.

COCONUT CARAMEL ICED COFFEE

Size: XL Multi-Serve setting
Brew: Over Ice
Makes: 1 (22-ounce) serving

INGREDIENTS

5 Ninja® Small Scoops
(or 5 tablespoons)
ground coconut coffee

2 cups ice

¼ cup caramel sauce

¼ cup half & half

DIRECTIONS

1. Following the measurement provided, place the ground coffee into the brew basket.

2. Place the ice, caramel sauce, and half & half into a 22-ounce or larger plastic cup; set cup in place to brew.

3. Select the XL Multi-Serve size; press the Over Ice Brew button.

4. When brew is complete, stir to combine.

PECAN CARAMEL ICED COFFEE

Size: Travel setting
Brew: Over Ice
Makes: 1 (16-ounce) serving

INGREDIENTS

4 Ninja® Small Scoops
(or 4 tablespoons)
ground pecan coffee

2 cups ice

2 tablespoons caramel syrup

2 tablespoons half & half

DIRECTIONS

1. Following the measurement provided, place the ground coffee into the brew basket.

2. Place the ice, caramel syrup, and half & half into a large plastic cup; set cup in place to brew.

3. Select the Travel size; press the Over Ice Brew button.

4. When brew is complete, stir to combine.

CREAMY CARAMEL ICED COFFEE

Size: Travel setting
Brew: Over Ice
Makes: 1 (16-ounce) serving

INGREDIENTS

4 Ninja® Small Scoops
(or 4 tablespoons) ground
French vanilla coffee

2 cups ice

1 tablespoon caramel syrup

1 tablespoon vanilla syrup

2 tablespoons half & half

DIRECTIONS

1. Following the measurement provided, place the ground coffee into the brew basket.

2. Place the ice, caramel syrup, vanilla syrup, and half & half into a large plastic cup; set cup in place to brew.

3. Select the Travel size; press the Over Ice Brew button.

4. When brew is complete, stir to combine.

LEMON CAYENNE ICED COFFEE

Size: Full Carafe setting
Brew: Over Ice
Makes: 4 (9-ounce) servings

INGREDIENTS

6 Ninja® Big Scoops
(or 12 tablespoons)
ground coffee

Zest of 1 lemon

$\frac{1}{4}$ teaspoon cayenne pepper

4 cups ice

$\frac{1}{4}$ teaspoon lemon juice

DIRECTIONS

1. Following the measurements provided, place the ground coffee, lemon zest, and cayenne pepper into the brew basket.

2. Place ice and lemon juice into the carafe; set carafe in place to brew.

3. Select the Full Carafe size; press the Over Ice Brew button.

4. When brew is complete, stir to combine. Pour coffee into 4 glasses.

CHOCOLATE CARAMEL NUT ICED COFFEE

Size: Travel setting
Brew: Over Ice
Makes: 1 (16-ounce) serving

INGREDIENTS

4 Ninja® Small Scoops
(or 4 tablespoons)
ground pecan coffee

2 cups ice

1 tablespoon chocolate syrup

1 tablespoon caramel syrup

2 tablespoons half & half

DIRECTIONS

1. Following the measurement provided, place the ground coffee into the brew basket.

2. Place the ice, chocolate syrup, caramel syrup, and half & half into a large plastic cup; set cup in place to brew.

3. Select the Travel size; press the Over Ice Brew button.

4. When brew is complete, stir to combine.

CHOCOLATE RASPBERRY ICED COFFEE

Size: Travel setting
Brew: Over Ice
Makes: 1 (16-ounce) serving

INGREDIENTS

4 Ninja® Small Scoops
(or 4 tablespoons)
ground chocolate
raspberry coffee

2 cups ice

2 tablespoons chocolate syrup

1/4 cup half & half

DIRECTIONS

1. Following the measurement provided, place the ground coffee into the brew basket.

2. Place the ice, chocolate syrup, and half & half into a large plastic cup; set cup in place to brew.

3. Select the Travel size; press the Over Ice Brew button.

4. When brew is complete, stir to combine.

ROSE & PISTACHIO ICED COFFEE

Size: XL Cup setting
Brew: Over Ice
Makes: 1 (16-ounce) serving

INGREDIENTS

3 Ninja® Small Scoops
(or 3 tablespoons)
ground coffee

1 cup ice

1 teaspoon sugar

½ teaspoon rosewater

½ cup pistachio ice cream

DIRECTIONS

1. Following the measurement provided, place the ground coffee into the brew basket.

2. Place the ice, sugar, rosewater, and ice cream into a large plastic cup; set cup in place to brew.

3. Select the XL Cup size; press the Over Ice Brew button.

4. When brew is complete, stir to combine.

YUAN YANG ICED COFFEE

Size: XL Multi-Serve setting
Brew: Over Ice
Makes: 1 (20-ounce) serving

INGREDIENTS

5 Ninja® Small Scoops
(or 5 tablespoons)
ground coconut coffee

1 tablespoon black tea leaves

2 ½ cups ice

¼ cup sweetened
condensed milk

DIRECTIONS

1. Following the measurements provided, place the ground coffee and black tea leaves into the brew basket.

2. Place the ice and sweetenedcondensed milk into a 22-ounce or larger plastic cup; set cup in place to brew.

3. Select the XL Multi-Serve size; press the Over Ice Brew button.

4. When brew is complete, stir to combine.

COFFEE SODA FLOAT

Size: Cup setting
Brew: Over Ice
Makes: 1 (12-ounce) serving

INGREDIENTS

For the Coffee Soda Concentrate:

3 Ninja® Small Scoops
(or 3 tablespoons)
ground coffee

$1/2$ cup sugar

For the float:

$1/4$ cup coffee soda concentrate
(recipe above)

$1/2$ cup vanilla ice cream

$3/4$ cup seltzer water

DIRECTIONS

1. Following the measurement provided, place the ground coffee into the brew basket.

2. Set a mug in place to brew.

3. Select the Cup size; press the Over Ice Brew button.

4. When brew is complete, make the coffee soda concentrate by combining the brewed coffee with sugar in a pan and cooking over high heat. Stir until sugar is dissolved, about 3 minutes. Allow to cool.

5. Pour the cooled coffee soda concentrate into a large glass. Add the vanilla ice cream and carefully pour in the seltzer water.

ICED VANILLA LATTE

SPECIALTY
(CONCENTRATED)
4oz

Brew: Specialty
Makes: 1 (16-ounce) serving

INGREDIENTS

2 Ninja® Big Scoops
(or 4 tablespoons)
ground coffee

2 tablespoons vanilla syrup

2 cups ice

$3/4$ cup milk

DIRECTIONS

1. Following the measurement provided, place the ground coffee into the brew basket.
2. Place vanilla syrup and ice into a large plastic cup; set cup in place to brew.
3. Press the Specialty button.
4. While coffee is brewing, place milk into a large mug.
5. When brew is complete, stir to combine.
6. Froth milk for 30 seconds according to frothing instructions in the Owner's Guide.
7. Gently pour frothed milk into coffee.

ICED CAPPUCCINO-STYLE COFFEE

Brew: Specialty
Makes: 1 (12-ounce) serving

INGREDIENTS

2 Ninja® Big Scoops
(or 4 tablespoons)
ground coffee

2 cups ice

½ cup milk

DIRECTIONS

1. Following the measurement provided, place the ground coffee into the brew basket.

2. Place the ice into a large plastic cup; set cup in place to brew.

3. Press the Specialty button.

4. While coffee is brewing, place milk into a mug.

5. When brew is complete, froth milk for 30 seconds according to frothing instructions in the Owner's Guide.

6. Gently pour frothed milk into coffee.

SPECIALTY
(CONCENTRATED)
4oz

ICED SOY LATTE

Brew: Specialty
Makes: 1 (16-ounce) serving

INGREDIENTS

2 Ninja® Big Scoops
(or 4 tablespoons)
ground coffee

2 cups ice

1/2 cup soy milk

DIRECTIONS

1. Following the measurement provided, place the ground coffee into the brew basket.
2. Place the ice into a large plastic cup; set cup in place to brew.
3. Press the Specialty button.
4. While coffee is brewing, place the soy milk into a large mug.
5. When brew is complete, froth milk for 30 seconds according to frothing instructions in the Owner's Guide.
6. Gently pour frothed milk into coffee.

SPECIALTY
(CONCENTRATED)
4oz

ICED AMERICANO

Brew: Specialty
Makes: 1 (12-ounce) serving

INGREDIENTS

2 Ninja® Big Scoops
(or 4 tablespoons)
ground coffee

2 cups ice

$\frac{1}{2}$ cup cold water,
plus more if desired

Milk and sugar, to taste

DIRECTIONS

1. Following the measurement provided, place the ground coffee into the brew basket.

2. Place the ice into a large plastic cup; set cup in place to brew.

3. Press the Specialty button.

4. When brew is complete, stir in the cold water; add milk and sugar to taste.

ICED COCONUT CHAI COFFEE

Brew: Specialty
Makes: 1 (16-ounce) serving

INGREDIENTS

2 Ninja® Big Scoops
(or 4 tablespoons)
ground coffee

$1/2$ teaspoon ground cinnamon

$1/4$ teaspoon ground nutmeg

$1/2$ teaspoon ground ginger

$1/2$ teaspoon ground cardamom

2 tablespoons vanilla syrup

2 cups ice

$3/4$ cup coconut milk

DIRECTIONS

1. Following the measurements provided, stir together the ground coffee, cinnamon, nutmeg, ginger, and cardamom; place into the brew basket.

2. Place vanilla syrup, ice, and coconut milk into a large plastic cup; set cup in place to brew.

3. Press the Specialty button.

4. When brew is complete, stir to combine.

ICED NUTTY COCOA LATTE

Brew: Specialty
Makes: 1 (18-ounce) serving

INGREDIENTS

2 Ninja® Big Scoops
(or 4 tablespoons)
ground coffee

2 tablespoons chocolate syrup,
plus more for garnish

1 tablespoon caramel syrup,
plus more for garnish

2 cups ice

½ cup milk

1 tablespoon peanut butter

DIRECTIONS

1. Following the measurement provided, place the ground coffee into the brew basket.

2. Place the chocolate syrup, caramel syrup, and ice into a large plastic cup; set cup in place to brew.

3. Press the Specialty button.

4. While coffee is brewing, place milk and peanut butter into a large mug and stir to combine.

5. When brew is complete, stir to combine.

6. Froth milk mixture for 30 seconds according to frothing instructions in the Owner's Guide.

7. Gently pour frothed mixture into coffee.

CARDAMOM VANILLA ICED LATTE

Brew: Specialty
Makes: 1 (16-ounce) serving

INGREDIENTS

2 Ninja® Big Scoops
(or 4 tablespoons)
ground coffee

$1/2$ teaspoon ground cardamom

2 cups ice

2 tablespoons vanilla syrup

$1/2$ cup milk

DIRECTIONS

1. Following the measurements provided, place the ground coffee and cardamom into the brew basket.

2. Place the ice and vanilla syrup into a large plastic cup; set cup in place to brew.

3. Press the Specialty button.

4. While coffee is brewing, place milk into a large mug.

5. When brew is complete, stir to combine.

6. Froth milk for 30 seconds according to frothing instructions in the Owner's Guide.

7. Gently pour frothed milk into coffee.

SPARKLING BUTTERSCOTCH COFFEE

Brew: Specialty
Makes: 1 (24-ounce) serving

INGREDIENTS

2 Ninja® Big Scoops
(or 4 tablespoons)
ground coffee

2 cups ice

2 tablespoons
butterscotch syrup

$1/8$ teaspoon salt

$1/8$ teaspoon vanilla extract

$1/4$ cup heavy cream

1 cup cream soda

DIRECTIONS

1. Following the measurement provided, place the ground coffee into the brew basket.

2. Place the ice, butterscotch syrup, salt, vanilla, and cream into a plastic cup; set cup in place to brew.

3. Press the Specialty button.

4. When brew is complete, stir to combine. Gently pour in cream soda.

SPECIALTY
(CONCENTRATED)
4oz

CLASSIC NINJACCINO™

Brew: Specialty
Makes: 2 (12-ounce) servings

INGREDIENTS

2 Ninja® Big Scoops
(or 4 tablespoons)
ground coffee

2 cups ice

$\frac{1}{4}$ cup milk

$\frac{1}{4}$ cup sweetened
condensed milk

DIRECTIONS

1. Following the measurement provided, place the ground coffee into the brew basket.

2. Place the ice into a large plastic cup; set cup in place to brew.

3. Press the Specialty button.

4. When brew is complete, combine coffee and ice with remaining ingredients in a 24-ounce or larger blender.

5. Blend until smooth, about 25 seconds.

6. Divide between 2 glasses.

DO NOT BLEND HOT INGREDIENTS.

SWEET SOFIACCINO

Brew: Specialty
Makes: 2 (10-ounce) servings

INGREDIENTS

2 Ninja® Big Scoops
(or 4 tablespoons)
ground coffee

3 cups ice

¼ cup evaporated milk

½ cup sweetened
condensed milk

Whipped cream,
for garnish

Ground cinnamon,
for garnish

DIRECTIONS

1. Following the measurement provided, place the ground coffee into the brew basket.

2. Place the ice into a large plastic cup; set cup in place to brew.

3. Press the Specialty button.

4. When brew is complete, combine coffee and ice with evaporated milk and sweetened condensed milk in a 24-ounce or larger blender.

5. Blend until smooth, about 25 seconds.

6. Divide between 2 glasses. Top with whipped cream and sprinkle with cinnamon.

DO NOT BLEND HOT INGREDIENTS.

SPECIALTY
(CONCENTRATED)
4oz

CINNAMON DULCE NINJACCINO™

Brew: Specialty
Makes: 2 (10-ounce) servings

INGREDIENTS

2 Ninja® Big Scoops
(or 4 tablespoons)
ground coffee

1/2 teaspoon ground cinnamon

3 cups ice

1/4 cup milk

1/2 cup dulce de leche

DIRECTIONS

1. Following the measurements provided, place the ground coffee and cinnamon into the brew basket.

2. Fill a large plastic cup with the ice; set cup in place to brew.

3. Press the Specialty button.

4. When brew is complete, combine coffee and ice with milk and dulce de leche in a 24-ounce or larger blender.

5. Blend until smooth, about 25 seconds; divide between 2 glasses.

DO NOT BLEND HOT INGREDIENTS.

SOFIA'S SIGNATURE

"This drink reminds me of my childhood combining two of my favorite things—coffee & dulce de leche."

Sofia

COCO-MOCHO CRUNCH NINJACCINO™

Brew: Specialty
Makes: 2 (12-ounce) servings

INGREDIENTS

2 Ninja® Big Scoops
(or 4 tablespoons)
ground coffee

3 cups ice

1/2 cup milk

1/4 cup chocolate syrup

3 tablespoons
toasted coconut, divided

Whipped cream,
for garnish

DIRECTIONS

1. Following the measurement provided, place the ground coffee into the brew basket.

2. Place the ice into a large plastic cup; set cup in place to brew.

3. Press the Specialty button.

4. When brew is complete, combine coffee and ice with milk, chocolate syrup, and 2 tablespoons toasted coconut in a 24-ounce or larger blender.

5. Blend until smooth, about 25 seconds.

6. Divide between 2 glasses. Top with whipped cream and sprinkle with remaining tablespoon of coconut.

DO NOT BLEND HOT INGREDIENTS.

PECAN PRALINE NINJACCINO™

SPECIALTY
(CONCENTRATED)
4oz

Brew: Specialty
Makes: 2 (10-ounce) servings

INGREDIENTS

2 Ninja® Big Scoops
(or 4 tablespoons)
ground coffee

3 cups ice

1/4 cup toasted pecans

1/4 cup milk

2 tablespoons butterscotch
or caramel sauce

2 tablespoons packed dark
brown sugar

1/4 teaspoon vanilla extract

DIRECTIONS

1. Following the measurement provided, place the ground coffee into the brew basket.

2. Place the ice into a large plastic cup; set cup in place to brew.

3. Press the Specialty button.

4. When brew is complete, combine coffee and ice with remaining ingredients in a 24-ounce or larger blender.

5. Blend until smooth, about 25 seconds.

6. Divide between 2 glasses.

DO NOT BLEND HOT INGREDIENTS.

COFFEE, COOKIES & CREAM FRAPPE

Brew: Specialty
Makes: 2 (8-ounce) servings

INGREDIENTS

2 Ninja® Big Scoops
(or 4 tablespoons)
ground coffee

2 cups ice

1/2 cup coffee ice cream

4 chocolate sandwich cookies,
plus 1 chopped for garnish

1/4 cup milk

Whipped cream, for garnish

DIRECTIONS

1. Following the measurement provided, place the ground coffee into the brew basket.

2. Place the ice into a large plastic cup; set cup in place to brew.

3. Press the Specialty button.

4. When brew is complete, combine coffee and ice with ice cream, cookies, and milk in a 24-ounce or larger blender.

5. Blend until smooth, about 25 seconds.

6. Divide between 2 glasses; top with whipped cream and chopped cookie.

DO NOT BLEND HOT INGREDIENTS.

S'MORES BRÛLÉE FRAPPE

Brew: Specialty
Makes: 1 (22-ounce) serving

INGREDIENTS

2 Ninja® Big Scoops
(or 4 tablespoons)
ground coffee

1 cup ice

1/2 cup mini marshmallows,
divided

1/2 cup milk

1/2 cup chocolate ice cream

3 whole graham crackers,
crushed, plus more for garnish

Chocolate syrup, for garnish

DIRECTIONS

1. Following the measurement provided, place the ground coffee into the brew basket.

2. Place the ice into a large plastic cup; set cup in place to brew.

3. Press the Specialty button.

4. Place marshmallows on a sheet pan under the broiler on high until deep golden, about 3 minutes. Set aside and let cool.

5. When brew is complete, combine coffee and ice with milk, ice cream, graham crackers, and half the marshmallows in a 24-ounce or larger blender.

6. Blend until smooth, about 30 seconds.

7. Top with remaining marshmallows, a drizzle of chocolate syrup, and crumbled graham crackers.

DO NOT BLEND HOT INGREDIENTS.

FROZEN PEPPERMINT MOCHA

Brew: Specialty
Makes: 2 (10-ounce) servings

INGREDIENTS

2 Ninja® Big Scoops
(or 4 tablespoons)
ground coffee

3 cups ice

$1/4$ cup coffee liqueur

2 tablespoons
peppermint schnapps

$1/4$ cup milk

2 tablespoons chocolate syrup

DIRECTIONS

1. Following the measurement provided, place the ground coffee into the brew basket.

2. Place the ice into a large plastic cup; set cup in place to brew.

3. Press the Specialty button.

4. When brew is complete, combine coffee and ice with remaining ingredients in a 24-ounce or larger blender.

5. Blend until smooth, about 25 seconds.

6. Divide between 2 glasses.

DO NOT BLEND HOT INGREDIENTS.

SPECIALTY
(CONCENTRATED)
4oz

MOCHA NINJACCINO™

Brew: Specialty
Makes: 2 (10-ounce) servings

INGREDIENTS

2 Ninja® Big Scoops
(or 4 tablespoons)
ground coffee

3 cups ice

$\frac{1}{4}$ cup milk

$\frac{1}{4}$ cup chocolate syrup,
plus more for garnish

Whipped cream, for garnish

DIRECTIONS

1. Following the measurement above, place the ground coffee into the brew basket.

2. Place the ice into a large plastic cup; set cup in place to brew.

3. Press the Specialty button.

4. When brew is complete, combine coffee and ice with milk and chocolate syrup in a 24-ounce or larger blender.

5. Blend until smooth, about 25 seconds.

6. Divide between 2 glasses. Top with whipped cream and drizzle with additional chocolate syrup.

DO NOT BLEND HOT INGREDIENTS.

CREAMY DREAMY VANILLA COCONUT NINJACCINO™

Brew: Specialty
Makes: 2 (12-ounce) servings

INGREDIENTS

2 Ninja® Big Scoops
(or 4 tablespoons)
ground coffee

3 cups ice

$1/3$ cup sweetened cream
of coconut

$1/4$ cup milk

1 teaspoon vanilla extract

$1/4$ cup toasted shredded
coconut, divided

Whipped cream, for garnish

DIRECTIONS

1. Following the measurement provided, place the ground coffee into the brew basket.
2. Place the ice into a large plastic cup; set cup in place to brew.
3. Press the Specialty button.
4. When brew is complete, combine coffee and ice with cream of coconut, milk, and vanilla in a 24-ounce or larger blender.
5. Blend until smooth, about 25 seconds. Stir in all but 1 teaspoon shredded coconut.
6. Divide between 2 glasses. Top with whipped cream and sprinkle with the remaining 1 teaspoon shredded coconut.

DO NOT BLEND HOT INGREDIENTS.

SPECIALTY
(CONCENTRATED)
4oz

IRISH STOUT COFFEE FLOAT

Brew: Specialty
Makes: 1 (20-ounce) serving

INGREDIENTS

2 Ninja® Big Scoops
(or 4 tablespoons)
ground coffee

2 cups ice

1 cup vanilla or
chocolate ice cream

1 cup Irish stout beer

DIRECTIONS

1. Following the measurement provided, place the ground coffee into the brew basket.

2. Place ice and ice cream into a large plastic cup; set cup in place to brew.

3. Press the Specialty button.

4. When brew is complete, gently pour in the stout beer. Stir to combine.

OVER ICE BREW

COFFEE NOG

Size: Cup setting
Brew: Over Ice
Makes: 2 (10-ounce) servings

INGREDIENTS

3 Ninja® Small Scoops
(or 3 tablespoons)
ground coffee

2–3 cups ice

¼ cup spiced rum

1 cup prepared eggnog

Ground nutmeg, for garnish

DIRECTIONS

1. Following the measurement provided, place the ground coffee into the brew basket.

2. Place the ice, rum, and eggnog into a plastic or metal cocktail shaker; set shaker in place to brew.

3. Select the Cup size; press the Over Ice Brew button.

4. When brew is complete, shake well to chill.

5. Strain and divide between 2 cups; sprinkle with nutmeg.

MEXICAN MOCHA MUDSLIDE

Brew: Specialty
Makes: 2 (11-ounce) servings

INGREDIENTS

2 Ninja® Big Scoops
(or 4 tablespoons)
ground coffee

2 cups ice

1 cup chocolate ice cream,
firmly packed

3 tablespoons coffee liqueur

3 tablespoons
dark crème de cacao

3 tablespoons vodka

$\frac{1}{4}$ teaspoon ground cinnamon

$\frac{1}{4}$ teaspoon chili powder

$\frac{1}{8}$ teaspoon cayenne pepper,
plus more for garnish

Whipped cream, for garnish

DIRECTIONS

1. Following the measurement provided, place the ground coffee into the brew basket.
2. Place the ice into a large plastic cup; set cup in place to brew.
3. Press the Specialty button.
4. When brew is complete, combine coffee and ice with remaining ingredients in a 24-ounce or larger blender.
5. Blend until smooth, about 25 seconds.
6. Divide between 2 glasses. Top with whipped cream and sprinkle with additional cayenne pepper.

DO NOT BLEND HOT INGREDIENTS.

DOUBLE-SHOT WHITE RUSSIAN

Size: Cup setting
Brew: Over Ice
Makes: 2 (5-ounce) servings

INGREDIENTS

3 Ninja® Small Scoops
(or 3 tablespoons)
ground coffee

2 cups ice

¼ cup vodka

¼ cup coffee liqueur

¼ cup heavy cream

DIRECTIONS

1. Following the measurement provided, place the ground coffee into the brew basket.

2. Place the ice into a plastic or metal cocktail shaker; set shaker in place to brew.

3. Select the Cup size; press the Over Ice Brew button.

4. When brew is complete, add vodka and coffee liqueur and shake well to chill.

5. Divide between 2 glasses, including ice, and top off each with heavy cream.

CAFE MARTINI

Size: Travel setting
Brew: Over Ice
Makes: 4 (4-ounce) servings

INGREDIENTS

4 Ninja® Small Scoops
(or 4 tablespoons)
ground coffee

2 cups ice

¼ cup coffee liqueur

¼ cup vodka

2 tablespoons
dark crème de cacao

¼ cup Irish cream

DIRECTIONS

1. Following the measurement provided, place the ground coffee into the brew basket.

2. Place the ice into a plastic or metal cocktail shaker; set shaker in place to brew.

3. Select the Travel size; press the Over Ice Brew button.

4. When brew is complete, add remaining ingredients and shake well to chill. Strain and divide between 4 glasses.

ALMOND CHOCOLATE-KISSED COFFEE COCKTAIL

Size: Cup setting
Brew: Over Ice
Makes: 2 (4-ounce) servings

INGREDIENTS

3 Ninja® Small Scoops
(or 3 tablespoons)
ground coffee

2 cups ice

2 tablespoons
amaretto liqueur

2 tablespoons
crème de cacao

Maraschino cherries,
for garnish

DIRECTIONS

1. Following the measurement provided, place the ground coffee into the brew basket.

2. Place the ice into a plastic or metal cocktail shaker; set shaker in place to brew.

3. Select the Cup size; press the Over Ice Brew button.

4. When brew is complete, add amaretto and crème de cacao and shake well to chill. Strain and divide between 2 glasses.

5. Garnish with maraschino cherries.

SOFIA'S SIGNATURE

"This cocktail is so smooth and delicious!"

Sofia

COFFEE OLD FASHIONED

Size: Travel setting
Brew: Over Ice
Makes: 2 (5-ounce) servings

INGREDIENTS

4 Ninja® Small Scoops
(or 4 tablespoons)
ground coffee

3 cups ice

3 tablespoons bourbon

1 tablespoon crème de cacao

1 tablespoon sugar

4 dashes bitters

2 strips orange peel,
for garnish

4 maraschino cherries,
for garnish

DIRECTIONS

1. Following the measurement provided, place the ground coffee into the brew basket.

2. Place the ice into a plastic or metal cocktail shaker; set shaker in place to brew.

3. Select the Travel size; press the Over Ice Brew button.

4. When brew is complete, add bourbon, crème de cacao, sugar, and bitters; shake well to chill.

5. Divide between 2 glasses, including ice, and garnish each with a piece of orange peel and 2 maraschino cherries.

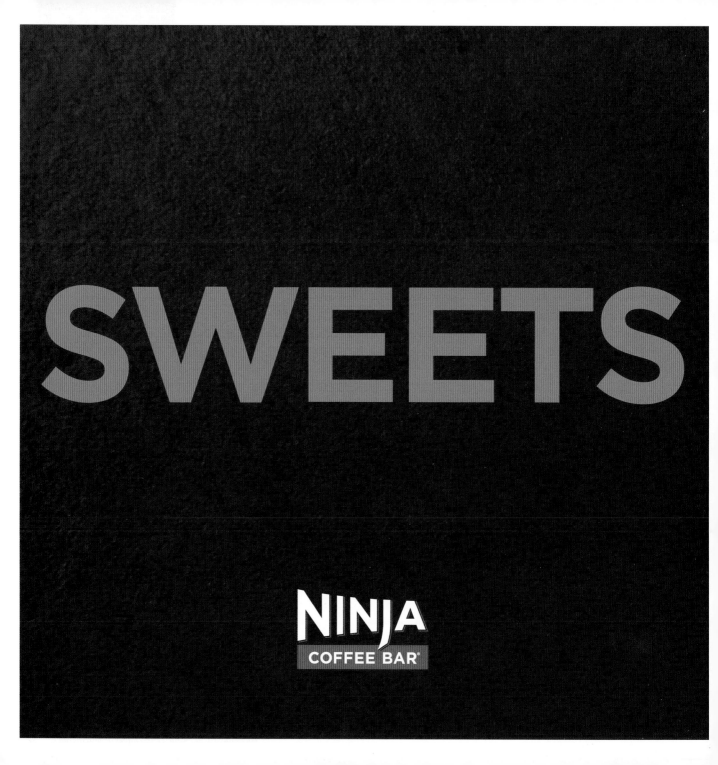

BASIC BISCOTTI

Prep time: 15 minutes
Cook time: 35 minutes
Makes: 24 biscotti

INGREDIENTS

2 cups all-purpose flour

1/2 teaspoon baking soda

1/2 teaspoon baking powder

1/4 teaspoon salt

1/2 cup (1 stick) unsalted butter, softened

1 cup granulated sugar

2 eggs

1 teaspoon vanilla

1 1/2–2 cups desired flavoring*

Flour, as needed

DIRECTIONS

1. Preheat oven to 350°F. Grease a cookie sheet; set aside.

2. Sift together flour, baking soda, baking powder, and salt; set aside.

3. Using an electric mixer, cream butter and sugar. Mix in eggs and vanilla. Add flour and desired flavorings* and mix to create dough.

4. Turn dough onto a lightly floured surface and divide into two equal portions. With lightly floured hands, roll dough to create a 12-inch long log and place on prepared cookie sheet. Repeat with remaining dough.

5. Bake 25 minutes or until golden brown. Remove from oven and let cool 10 minutes.

6. Cut log diagonally into 1-inch cookies (12 per log). Place biscotti base-side down on the cookie sheet and bake for 10 to 12 more minutes. Cool biscotti and place in a cookie tin. Biscotti can be stored up to 1 week at room temperature or frozen for 2 to 3 months.

*Flavoring ideas

Almond Anise: Add 2 cups toasted chopped almonds and 1 teaspoon anise seed.

Orange Hazelnut: Add 2 cups toasted chopped hazelnuts and 1 tablespoon orange zest.

Chocolate Hazelnut: Add 2 cups toasted chopped hazelnuts and 3 ounces melted chocolate.

Cranberry, Lime, and Pistachio: Add 1 tablespoon lime zest, 1/2 cup shelled pistachios, and 1/2 cup dried cranberries.

CRUMB CAKE

Prep time: 30 minutes   **Rise time:** 2 hours 30 minutes
Cook time: 35–40 minutes
Makes: 12 servings

INGREDIENTS

Dough:

1 cup whole milk, warm

$1/2$ cup granulated sugar

1 package (2 $1/2$ teaspoons) instant yeast

2 eggs

$1/2$ cup (1 stick) butter, melted

4 $1/2$ cups all-purpose flour

1 $1/2$ teaspoons salt

Topping:

1 cup dark brown sugar, packed

$1/4$ cup granulated sugar

2 tablespoons ground cinnamon

1 $1/2$ teaspoons salt

1 cup (2 sticks) butter, softened

3 cups all-purpose flour

Powdered sugar, for garnish

DIRECTIONS

1. To prepare dough, combine milk, sugar, and yeast in a large bowl, whisking until yeast is evenly distributed. Add eggs, butter, flour, and salt. Stir until a slightly sticky dough is created. Dough should pull away from the bowl. Add additional flour if needed.

2. Using well-floured hands or a rubber spatula, knead dough for 3 to 5 minutes. Cover bowl with plastic wrap and set in a warm place to rise for 2 hours, or until dough has almost doubled in size.

3. After the dough has risen, press it evening into a parchment-lined and well-greased 11x11-inch or larger deep-dish baking pan.

4. In a small bowl, stir together all ingredients for crumb topping until well combined. Using your hands, grab small handfuls of topping firmly to form large crumbs. Place crumbs on top of dough until all dough is coated evenly with crumbs. Allow dough to rise for an additional 30 minutes in a warm place. Meanwhile, preheat oven to 350°F.

5. Bake crumb cake 35 to 40 minutes, or until a wooden toothpick inserted in center comes out clean. Allow to cool completely in pan, then sprinkle with powdered sugar before serving.

MAPLE PECAN SCONES

Prep time: 15 minutes
Cook time: 15–17 minutes
Makes: 8 scones

INGREDIENTS

2 cups all-purpose or bread flour

1/4 cup granulated sugar

1 teaspoon baking powder

1/4 teaspoon baking soda

1/4 teaspoon salt

1/2 cup (1 stick) unsalted butter, very cold, cut in small cubes

1 1/4 cups chopped pecans, divided

1/2 cup sour cream

1/2 cup maple syrup, divided

1 large egg

1 cup confectioners' sugar

DIRECTIONS

1. Preheat oven to 400°F.

2. Using an electric mixer with paddle attachment, mix flour, sugar, baking powder, baking soda, and salt.

3. Add butter and mix on low until well incorporated and pea-sized, about 2 minutes.

4. Add 1 cup pecans, sour cream, 1/4 cup maple syrup, and egg and mix just until dough forms, about 30 seconds.

5. Form dough into a ball, then place on a nonstick or lightly floured surface. Press dough to create a flat, round 7-inch disk. Cut disk into 8 equal pieces.

6. Place scones on a nonstick baking sheet. Bake 15 to 17 minutes, or until bottom edges are golden. Cool completely.

7. Stir together remaining 1/4 cup maple syrup with confectioners' sugar to form a glaze. Drizzle scones with glaze and sprinkle with remaining 1/4 cup pecans.

BLUEBERRY STREUSEL MUFFINS

Prep time: 15 minutes
Cook time: 25–30 minutes
Makes: 12 muffins

INGREDIENTS

Muffins:

2 cups flour

1 teaspoon baking soda

¼ teaspoon salt

½ cup (1 stick) unsalted butter, room temperature

¾ cup granulated sugar

2 eggs

1 teaspoon vanilla extract

1 cup buttermilk

1 ½ cups fresh or frozen blueberries

Streusel topping:

1 cup flour

¼ cup granulated sugar

½ teaspoon ground cinnamon

6 tablespoons butter, melted

DIRECTIONS

1. Preheat oven to 350°F. Mix together flour, baking soda, and salt in a bowl; set aside.

2. Using an electric mixer with a paddle attachment, cream the butter. Then add sugar gradually and beat until light and fluffy. Add eggs, one at a time, and then vanilla extract.

3. Alternately add buttermilk and flour mixture. Mix until smooth. Stir in the blueberries. Transfer the batter to a lined muffin pan.

4. To make the streusel topping, mix together the flour, sugar, cinnamon, and melted butter with a wooden spoon. Sprinkle 2 tablespoons of topping on each muffin.

5. Bake 25 to 30 minutes or until a wooden toothpick inserted in the center of a muffin comes out clean. Transfer muffins to a wire rack and cool completely.

FROSTED RUM PECAN CINNAMON BUNS

Prep time: 30 minutes   **Rise time:** 2 hours 30 minutes
Cook time: 15 minutes
Makes: 12 rolls

INGREDIENTS

Dough:

1 cup whole milk, warm

1/2 cup granulated sugar

1 packet (2 1/2 teaspoons) instant yeast

2 eggs

1/2 cup (1 stick) butter, melted

4 1/2 cups all-purpose flour

1 1/2 teaspoons salt

Filling:

1/3 cup butter, softened

1 cup dark brown sugar, packed

2 1/2 tablespoons ground cinnamon

Cream Cheese Frosting:

1 package (8 ounces) cream cheese, softened

2 cups confectioners' sugar

1/4 teaspoon vanilla extract

1/8 teaspoon salt (optional)

Rum Pecan Topping:

1/4 cup (1/2 stick) butter, melted

1/4 cup dark brown sugar

1/4 teaspoon ground cinnamon

1 tablespoon spiced rum

1/8 teaspoon salt

1 cup toasted pecans

DIRECTIONS

1. To prepare dough, combine milk, sugar, and yeast in a large bowl, whisking until yeast is evenly distributed. Add eggs, butter, flour, and salt. Stir until a slightly sticky dough is created. Dough should pull away from the bowl. Add additional flour if needed.

2. Using well-floured hands or a rubber spatula, knead the dough for 3 to 5 minutes. Cover bowl with plastic wrap and set in a warm place to rise for 2 hours, or until it has almost doubled in size. After the dough has risen, place it on a lightly floured surface. Allow dough to rest for a few minutes.

3. Preheat oven to 400°F.

4. In a small bowl, combine brown sugar and cinnamon for the filling; set aside.

5. Roll out dough into a 12x18-inch rectangle, then create the filling by spreading dough evenly with butter then sprinkling with cinnamon-sugar mixture. Roll up dough into a cylinder and then cut it into 12 rolls, each about an inch wide. Place rolls in a lightly greased or parchment-lined 9x13-inch baking pan, spiral facing up. Cover and let rise until nearly doubled in size, about 30 minutes.

6. Bake rolls for 15 minutes, or until golden brown.

7. While rolls are baking, beat together all ingredients for cream cheese frosting in a small bowl; set aside.

8. In a separate bowl, combine all ingredients for pecan topping, except the pecans. Microwave topping mixture for 30 seconds, then add pecans and stir until combined.

9. Spread frosting on hot rolls and top with pecan topping. Allow to cool at least 20 minutes before serving warm.

BACON & SPINACH QUICHE

Prep time: 20 minutes
Cook time: 1 hour
Makes: 1 quiche (8 servings)

INGREDIENTS

1/2 pound sliced bacon (about 6 strips)

1/4 cup red onion, thinly sliced

1 clove garlic, minced

5 large eggs, slightly beaten

2 cups heavy cream

1 1/2 cups shredded Gruyère cheese, divided

1 cup baby spinach, chopped

1/2 teaspoon salt

1/8 teaspoon ground black pepper

1/8 teaspoon cayenne pepper

1 prepared pie crust

DIRECTIONS

1. Preheat oven to 425°F.

2. In a large nonstick skillet, cook bacon slices over medium-high heat about 5 minutes, or until golden and crispy. Transfer to a plate lined with paper towel. Remove all but 1 tablespoon bacon fat from pan. Add onion and cook until translucent, about 3 minutes. Add garlic and stir for 30 seconds. Remove from heat.

3. In a large bowl, mix eggs, cream, 1 cup cheese, spinach, salt, black pepper, and cayenne pepper.

4. Place pie crust into a quiche or pie dish. Crumble bacon and spread evenly along bottom of crust. Add onion and garlic mixture. Add remaining cheese. Pour egg mixture over the crust and gently stir to incorporate ingredients.

5. Bake quiche for 10 minutes. Then reduce heat to 325°F and cook for an additional 50 minutes or until crust is golden and filling is set. Allow to stand 20 minutes before serving.

SOUR CREAM COFFEE CAKE

Prep time: 15 minutes
Cook time: 1 hour
Makes: 1 cake (16 servings)

INGREDIENTS

Crumb topping:

2 cups pecans, roughly chopped

1 cup light brown sugar, firmly packed

1 cup all-purpose flour

$1/2$ cup (1 stick) unsalted butter, melted

1 tablespoon cinnamon

$1/2$ teaspoon salt

Cake:

2 $1/2$ cups all-purpose flour

1 teaspoon baking powder

1 teaspoon baking soda

$1/2$ teaspoon salt

1 cup granulated sugar

1 cup (2 sticks) unsalted butter, cut in pieces

1 $1/2$ cups sour cream

3 large eggs

1 tablespoon vanilla extract

DIRECTIONS

1. Preheat oven to 350°F. Butter a 10-inch tube pan.

2. In a large bowl, mix together all ingredients for the crumb topping; set aside.

3. In a medium bowl, combine flour, baking powder, baking soda, and salt; set aside.

4. Using an electric mixer on low-medium speed, cream granulated sugar and butter until fluffy. Add sour cream, eggs, and vanilla, then continue mixing, about 3 minutes. Scrape down sides of bowl as needed. Mixture will be chunky.

5. Add dry ingredients and continue to mix until thick batter comes together.

6. Layer $1/2$-inch of batter into tube pan, spreading it gently along the bottom and sides. Sprinkle in half the crumb mixture, then evenly layer the remaining cake batter on top. Top cake with remaining crumb mixture.

7. Bake 1 hour, or until wooden toothpick inserted in center of cake comes out clean. Allow cake to cool completely before removing from pan.

APPLE FRITTER CAKE

Prep time: 15 minutes
Cook time: 45 minutes
Makes: 1 cake (16 servings)

INGREDIENTS

2 cups flour

1 ½ cups granulated sugar

1 tablespoon baking powder

1 tablespoon ground cinnamon

1 teaspoon salt

½ cup milk

2 eggs

¼ cup (½ stick) unsalted butter, melted

2 teaspoons vanilla extract

1 apple, peeled, finely chopped

Confectioners' sugar, for dusting

DIRECTIONS

1. Preheat oven to 350°F. Grease a 12-inch Bundt pan.

2. Combine flour, sugar, baking powder, cinnamon, and salt in a bowl and mix thoroughly.

3. In a separate bowl, mix together milk, eggs, melted butter, vanilla, and apple.

4. Add wet ingredients to dry ingredients and mix until a thick batter forms.

5. Pour batter evenly into prepared pan.

6. Bake 45 minutes or until a wooden toothpick inserted in center comes out clean. Allow to cool, then remove from pan and flip over. Dust with confectioners' sugar.

CLASSIC TIRAMISU

Prep time: 30 minutes   **Cook time:** 4 minutes   **Chill time:** 4–24 hours
Brew: Specialty
Makes: 8–12 servings

INGREDIENTS

3 Ninja® Big Scoops
(or 6 tablespoons)
ground coffee

6 large egg yolks

$\frac{1}{2}$ cup granulated sugar

2 cups mascarpone cheese

2 cups heavy whipping cream

1 cup coffee liqueur

2 packages (4.7 ounces each)
lady finger cookies

1 heaping tablespoon
unsweetened cocoa powder,
placed in a small sieve or
strainer for dusting

DIRECTIONS

1. Following the measurement provided, place the ground coffee into the brew basket.

2. Set a small bowl in place to brew.

3. Press the Specialty button. When brew is complete, allow coffee to cool.

4. While coffee is cooling, prepare a double boiler.* Add egg yolks and sugar to the double boiler. Whisk constantly for 4 minutes, or until egg yolk is light yellow with a smooth, creamy, melted marshmallow texture. Remove from heat.

5. Whisk mascarpone cheese into egg yolk mixture.

6. In a separate large bowl, mix heavy whipping cream with 2 tablespoons cooled, brewed coffee. Whip until soft peaks form.

7. Add coffee liqueur to remaining brewed coffee.

8. Assemble the tiramisu by dipping lady fingers one at a time into coffee liqueur mixture and placing in an even layer at the bottom of a trifle bowl or ceramic dish. Spread $\frac{1}{3}$ of the mascarpone-egg mixture onto lady fingers, followed by $\frac{1}{3}$ whipped cream, followed by a dusting of cocoa powder. Repeat layers again, starting with coffee-dipped lady fingers. The final layer should be whipped cream, topped with an even dusting of cocoa powder.

9. Chill in refrigerator 4 to 24 hours before serving.

If you don't have a double boiler, use a small pot full of almost simmering water topped with a large metal bowl.

LEMON BARS

Prep time: 20 minutes
Cook time: 35–40 minutes
Makes: 12 servings

INGREDIENTS

2 sticks (1 cup) unsalted butter, softened

2 cups granulated sugar, divided

2 $\frac{1}{3}$ cups all-purpose flour, divided

4 large eggs

$\frac{2}{3}$ cup lemon juice

Confectioners' sugar, for dusting

DIRECTIONS

1. Preheat oven to 350°F.

2. Place butter, $\frac{1}{2}$ cup sugar, and 2 cups flour into the bowl of a food processor fitted with a dough blade. Pulse until dough just comes together.

3. Press dough into the bottom of an ungreased 9x13-inch baking dish. Bake 15 minutes or until firm and golden in color. Cool for 10 minutes.

4. Clean the food processor bowl, then add remaining sugar, remaining flour, eggs, and lemon juice. Process until smooth.

5. Pour lemon mixture over par-baked crust. Bake 20 to 25 minutes. Lemon bars will be soft after baking, but will firm as they cool.

6. Cool completely, then dust with confectioners' sugar.

SALTY CHOCOLATE CHUNK COOKIES

Prep time: 15 minutes
Cook time: 12 minutes
Makes: 12 large or 24 small cookies

INGREDIENTS

1 $1/2$ cups all-purpose flour

1 teaspoon baking powder

$1/4$ teaspoon baking soda

2 teaspoons salt

$1/2$ cup (1 stick) unsalted butter, room temperature

1 cup dark brown sugar, packed

$1/2$ cup granulated sugar

2 eggs

2 teaspoons vanilla extract

8 ounces bittersweet chocolate, cut in small chunks

1 cup chopped walnuts

Large-crystal sea salt, for garnish

DIRECTIONS

1. Preheat oven to 375°F. Lightly grease 2 large cookie sheets; set aside.

2. In a small bowl, combine flour, baking powder, baking soda, and salt; set aside.

3. Using an electric mixer with paddle attachment, cream butter, brown sugar, and granulated sugar until light and fluffy. Add eggs and vanilla, and mix until combined. Add flour mixture and mix just until dough forms.

4. Mix in chocolate chunks and walnuts until well incorporated.

5. Scoop out 12 large (or 24 small) heaps of dough onto cookie sheets, spacing them at least 2 inches apart. Flatten slightly.

6. Sprinkle cookies with large-crystal sea salt, then bake for 12 minutes or until edges are golden brown. Allow cookies to cool slightly before moving to wire racks to cool completely.

CHOCOLATE RASPBERRY AFFOGATO

Prep time: 5 minutes
Brew: Specialty
Makes: 4 servings

INGREDIENTS

4 Ninja® Small Scoops
(or 4 tablespoons) ground
chocolate raspberry coffee

2 cups vanilla gelato or ice cream

¼ cup chocolate syrup

½ cup fresh raspberries,
for garnish

DIRECTIONS

1. Following the measurement provided, place the ground coffee into the brew basket.

2. Set a mug in place to brew

3. Press the Specialty button.

4. While coffee is brewing, divide gelato between 4 small cups or ice cream dishes.

5. Pour brewed coffee over the gelato in each cup, then top with chocolate syrup and garnish with raspberries.

INDEX

SWEETS